Where the Spirit Meets the Bones

Alyssa Hockett

BookLeaf Publishing

India | USA | UK

Presentation by *BookLeaf Publishing*

Web: www.bookleafpub.com

E-mail: info@bookleafpub.com

ISBN: 9789358319194

First edition 2023

DEDICATION

To my mom, my forever best friend and biggest supporter.

To my dad, who taught me what it means to be strong.

To my nana, who taught me what it means to be kind.

To my sisters, once girls together, soul mates forever, SSS.

To my friends, who make even the bad days worth it.

To my Skyylar, who motivates me to be my best.

To myself, you did it.

ACKNOWLEDGEMENT

Thank you to BookLeaf Publishing for giving me this once-in-a-lifetime experience and making a 20-something's dream come true.
I'd like to recognize the work of AI with my book's cover, for in part helping create the artwork with my input.

PREFACE

With love, light, and wanderlust, I hope you
enjoy exploring this book.

Survived.

I think there's something in that
when eulogies are written,
they almost always describe people as who they
were to others.
It says they're "survived by them,"
and I just think it's beautiful,
that to know someone is to know who they love.

And I'd like to think that when it's my time,
well darling, they'd have to start with you.

The Mourning After.

They say grief is just love in a heavy coat,
so when she stops me in the middle of a busy
street, on a beautiful sunny day,
and she tells me to get inside,
insists "it's going to rain,"

I tell her that it's okay.
All the love that she carried remains,
she can take off her heavy coat and shades
and bask in the sunlight once more.

The lessons learned, the memories earned,
that is all still loved.

The Mourning After II.

And I still remember,
the first night you came over,
you laid next to me talking for hours.

Then you asked me something,
and before I could finish,
you pulled me in,
god I still feel it.

Awake until sunrise, still, you held me close,
you whispered to me, "I don't want you to go,"
the most charming boy,
one I used to know.

Then the winter came, as quick as the day.
And sure you stuck around, but you didn't stay.

So in the morning after,
I'll keep mourning after
all the wasted love
and leftover laughter.

Come Back Halley, 1986.

I remember writing to Venus,
and pleading to the moon that night,
they said we can't force the stars to align,
so no matter how many tears I cried,
we were meant to fail by design.

And when I asked the supernovas which of us
would explode first,
the answer was in their silence.
I knew from that moment we were cursed.

Because Jupiter's gravity can redirect meteors
from Earth,
but it can't pull you any closer to me.

And all my prayers to Saturn,
but she'll be the only one with a ring.

So call me cliché, but when they'll ask me who's
to blame, it'll be "the galaxy," I say.

Because there's no way that this wasn't a cosmic
intervention,
the stars that sparkled in your eyes were never
on our side.
With you, there was never any question,
but I see now that the constellations had lied.

So I'll curse Orion, Cassiopeia, everything
between,
and I'll blame it on the stars,
since we were only nineteen.

Serendipity.

Before you I used to believe I could write about
heartbreak like it was pouring out of my
fingertips,
It's in the ink dripping from my pen,
spilling out like blood from my back.
And yet, I still can't describe the way you
touched me.

No list of beautiful words,
however carefully stringed together,
could ever recapture the feeling you gave to me
that night.

And as if love wasn't the greatest mastermind
plan of the whole entire universe,
then it's still pretty amazing that we found it all
on our own,
even if only for a short moment in time.

Wales - A Dedication to Aberystwyth.

The pier stretches out, afar from the bay.
She stands strong and tall, even on the windiest
of days.

And on the stormiest of nights, they say you can
feel the waves.
The pressure on the pier, swaying to remind us
of the dance between land and sea.
Oh, how lively it is, with its moonlit dancing and
afternoon tea,
it holds memories, that one day only it will
remember.

The friendliest of souls, a place to call home,
where dragons and dreams fly, and sheep roam,
Yn my nghalon am byth.
(In my heart forever).

Syndrome.

Sometimes it feels like my dream world and the real world are colliding.
I took a flight last night, though I'm not sure where.
But I had my water bottle, the one I lost the cap to, somehow it was there.

A water bottle without a cap is a liability.

I wonder if we lose things to this other side,
like a dark void, tranquility,
only found in this phantom city.
I only ever see you in these dreams anymore,
with your face all morphed,
and I can't remember how it was before.

But I've figured it out now,
we're in Stockholm again,
and nobody knows anything you ever did to me.
It's June, I should be grateful for the sunlight,
yet I'm praying to speak to the moon.
I'll tell her,
"People can be liabilities too."

And as she pulls the waves further from me,
and I chase the tide out to sea,
I wake up before I even realize I was dreaming,
and I thank her, that you're not next to me.

What I Needed to Hear.

Sweetheart, I know.
Everything they've done has left you
questioning everything they are,
everything you were.

You don't have to forgive them.
You don't have to forget.
You don't have to do anything, except,
accept.

Accept that people change, or they don't,
but the only change that matters is that change
inside of yourself.
Accept the good days with the bad.
Accept the heartbreak with the love you had.
And trust, you will be okay.

Faithless.

I always knew Rome wasn't built overnight,
and neither are good men.
So when you came back, I should have known,
I loved what you could have been.

And losing you was like losing my religion,
having all the faith and hope in my body,
picked and plucked out of me.
My god was a renegade, and I, a hopeless
martyr.

This was when I learned,
that sacrifice is not always beautiful or poetic,
and salvation isn't always earned.

Faith.

12

I am not one to tell you that you must believe in
something or someone or someplace specific.
But I will tell you that you must believe.
Be it in yourself, in a god, in the universe, in
your dog.
Believe in your best friend,
believe in karma,
believe that everything that's meant to, will
mend.

Noodles.

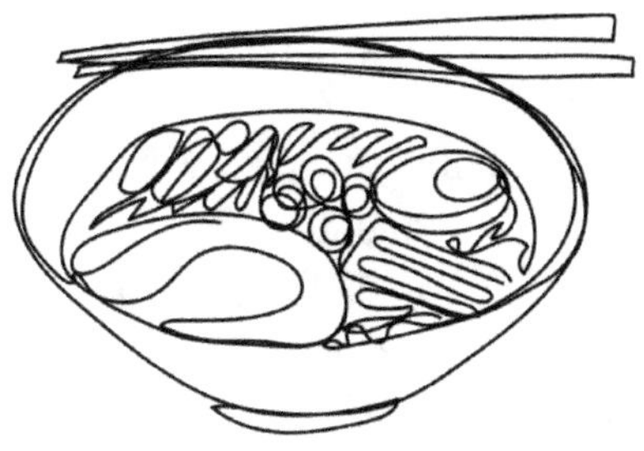

It's not the big memories I find myself
frequenting,
It's the 2ams in your kitchen, rummaging
through your cupboard.
You stand towering behind me, hands against
my hips.
Hungry for more than the food we're standing
before,
I'd turn around and look up into your eyes
before leaning into your lips.

"Noodles?" you asked.
It was these small moments that I wish could
last.

And even though I hated the spicy flavors, I
went home that next morning and stopped at the
small convenience shop on the corner.
Buying all your favorites in hopes that the taste
left off on my lips would be enough to keep you
around.

But now I keep them tucked away in the back of
my cabinet, out of sight,
so that I'm not reminded that you prefer fresh
fruit and fine wine now.
Don't get me wrong, I reach for the Rosé every
night I hear you're back in town.
And something about sweet strawberries
reminds me of our last kiss.

But still, some nights I find myself at 2am,
reaching for those last remnants I have of you,
and savoring every last bite.

Hell Hath No Fury.

15

And I wonder,
of all the vampires and werewolves
that come out at night,
and all the hunters that search for them,
and the towns that fear them.

What they would do when the moonlight
shined on a woman scorned?

Ivy - Inspired by Taylor Swift.

Happiness wraps around me like ivy,
it seeps into my every pore
like the sunlight on my skin.
Watching the trees in the wind
how they look so lively,
I know that to just acknowledge life
is the ultimate win.

And I know deep down, where my spirit meets
my bone, all will be okay, to let it be,
as long as the sun is shining another day,
the sea still moves for me.

Sometimes the world can feel like it's stopped
spinning,
and there's nothing more you'd like to do than
hop off, start your new beginning,
but Earth is so sweet to us, so kind and soft,
if you take a look around,
it might be nice to stay awhile.

My Atlantis - Inspired by Seafret.

So when my eyes get puffy
and the tears start to fall,
I'll notice the taste of my sorrows
and how it matches that of the sea I had to sail
across to meet you.
I'm grateful to have known you.

And I think I was in love,
for what I knew love to be at the time.

But I learned that, eventually,
the tide washes over every handmade heart of
sand.
And like how my love for you washed over me,
I was drowning.
(and I think maybe you were too,
but you'd choke on your own tears,
before asking for help)

And so, only in that last desperate gasp for air,
and only then, no time there after.

I'll keep searching for you,
my magical,
ancient,
great,
Love.
My Atlantis.

Id, Ego, and You.

No, no,
I will not apologize.
You don't ask a kid who scraped his knee
why he's bleeding.
So you don't get to ask me,
why I'm still crying.
I'm in mourning,
mourning who I thought you were.

And mourning doesn't know time,
unlike the neverending hours of night.

There are moments I'm afraid I'll spend my
whole life grieving,
but there are also moments when the sun comes
up, and moments when I see my friends.
There are still cups of tea that need pouring and
miracles that need believing.

I think, if I truly knew today was my last day on
earth,
I would still swallow my pride and want to
spend it with you.
even if that means never getting an "I'm sorry."

but this isn't my last day,
and you might be sorry but I'll never hear it.
Ego is a hell of a drug.

Sisterhood.

The love I have for the women and girls in my life is something no poem could ever put into words.

I like to imagine us together in every lifetime, as some sheep playing in the herd, or flying side by side as a couple of mockingbirds.

And in every lifetime, when the wind becomes turbulent, or the grass isn't as green, you'd still be beside me.

Eastgate Haunting.

There's way too many ghosts at this party,
too many old faces and too many signs,
on my sixth drink and it's only 6:30,
got me finishing a whole bottle of wine.

Because we died four months ago
but seeing you now feels like our wake,
and sure we've both grown,
but we can't unbury this grave.

It's every time I'm on Eastgate,
and I'm drinking my night away,
I'll see you walking in, with your friends, but we
both know that it's way too late.
And it kills me every time because we both
know that it's not your taste.
I think there's a haunting on Eastgate.

But regardless I try, ignore those daunting eyes,
thought I left your shadow in my room.
But then you walk by, keep your head down low,
you keep dodging me as if they don't know…
about you and me, but now it seems we're over.
I guess this is my closure.
...

But how can you just stand there?
With your new friends,
and same baggy hair,
you sit next to me but don't say hi,
gave you all my love to make me the bad guy?

Because the man I knew,
what we went through,
all those sleepless nights, the kiss goodbye,
they flash back to me,
the coldest memory.
So either this is fate,
Or there's a haunting on Eastgate.

Picasso.

I used to think you were my soulmate,
now I curse the God I don't even believe in
that he ever led me to you,
his unholiest saint, who had his complex.
Red like the tint on my lips
matching the bruise on his neck,
the taste of your own medicine you couldn't
take.

You painted me the devil,
yet with every stroke,
your brush revealed another infidelity.
What artist can't settle their own shaking hand?
Staring down the eyes of their masterpiece?

Never Fall For a Casual Drinker.

Because you will never understand regret,
until you know what it's like to pour all of
yourself into someone,
only for them to say they're not thirsty anymore.

You don't know what it's like to sacrifice a drop,
meanwhile I sacrifice my own blood
every time I taste the iron filling my mouth
when I lie through my teeth, and say,
"Sorry, I don't know him."

And I hate that it's months later,
and I'm still in my "healing journey,"
or whatever term of the week I'm using
to excuse the fact that I still miss you,
when I know I shouldn't.

I hate that I've now missed you for far longer
than I got to hold you.
It was the type of young love,
that never made its way around the sun.
Twelve weeks,
that's all there ever was of you and me.

So is it really strange that your absence has
changed me
far more than your presence did?
To love you was painful,
and I, a masochist.
Yet I can't regret you, and I won't.
I would do it all again.

But some days I wonder,
if we had met in the summer,
under the warm July breeze,
would it have gone any better?

Love from Across the Pond.

And so I must love you as though I love the sun,
with great admiration, fondness, and gratitude,
but never so close.

The second hardest thing you could ever be
asked of,
is to go out into the world and find yourself.
The first hardest,
knowing when to come back.

But this life is yours for the taking,
and if you don't someone else will for you,
sometimes you only notice a dream when you're
awaking,
And life is a dream too.

So when it's the end of the night and I'm
walking myself home,
I'll find myself looking up, under the same
moon,
asking each individual star if they could shine a
little brighter,
just for you.

Lost in Venice.

It was only when I started following the lantern
lights and midnight canals,
wandering, lost, in the floating city,
I realized I had finally found myself.

There is a great, giant world out there.
There are great, giant hearts out there.
You may go your whole life without ever really
meeting yourself,
and that would be the biggest tragedy of your
story.
So go get lost, in Venice, Vienna, wherever calls
to your bones.
Get lost in your best friend's room, you don't
have to be alone.

It is only when you look in a mirror and realize
that you'll always be home,
that then you will give life and your heart their
chance to roam.

Price of Your Pride.

In the end you may have been right,
but that doesn't mean that you were good.

The Physics of Love.

Sometimes I feel like we're tied together,
like I can't get away from you,
despite being so far away, for far too long.

I wonder if I can feel your pain,
and that's why I get a heaviness weighing on my
chest on a random Tuesday.
Or if you can hear the sound of my cries
fading out in the back of your mind.

There's this theory called quantum
entanglement.
The idea that two particles living across the
universe can be connected, energetically bound
as one.

The idea that you could put an entire galaxy
between you and me,
and our bodies would still feel each other,
deep in the soul of our every atom.

So just remember this…

You could fly to the other side of the Earth,
trying to outrun what you know is my worth.

Or travel across the whole wide universe,
thinking that my love is a curse.
But once you have known
the unconditional love of a woman, how it takes
shape,
you'll know that its presence is something
you will never be able to escape.

Sanctuary.

But you'll come to see,
little miss twenty something,
that the biggest monsters
aren't the ones that crawl out from under our
bed,
they're the ones that are invited into it.

Mind your sanctuary.

Fine Line

How can Jupiter pull meteors away from Earth,
but still can't pull this anger out of me?

And I often wonder, who are we,
when stripped bare of our humanity?

Those that have seen my darkest hatred
have also known my most sacred love.

Candles.

Happy birthday.
I do mean it.
I hope it's a good day, a great day, even,
and you get everything you ever dreamed of.

I hope you get that top executive career, the
fancy car.
I hope the night shines bright,
and you get to see every last star.
I hope you travel the world to see the seven
wonders,
but then can't help but wonder, about the eighth,
and if it was me?

I always told you I wished you the best,
and I meant it,
but I hope it's never enough.
I hope the void of me dilutes your wildest
dreams,
and you wish you had treated me differently.

Happy birthday.
I hope your wishes come true,
and that you're careful what you wish for.

Justice.

I think, in hindsight, you were right.
We couldn't be together anymore,
especially not after what you did.
I'm someone that believes in justice, in karma,
in the powers of balance in the universe.

The things you did to me, the betrayal,
dishonesty,
the entire fabrication of the man I thought I
loved.
I could never repay you for that.
I could never give you the justice that the world
and I will now demand from you.

Sure, you had to let me go, for your own
reasons,
but I had to let you go, so the universe could
deliver to you all the karma that I couldn't,
because I loved you.

And if losing a woman who loved you this
deeply isn't justice enough, I trust the universe
will deliver the rest.

Legacy

If my words could immortalize you,
you would have never died.
I don't know who you are today,
but I knew who you were back then.
Trying on new personalities
like we're playing pretend.
You said you're living for your legacy,
so with me will live and die our memory.

Heaven is on Earth.

Sometimes I like to imagine I just died,
and I'm revisiting Earth again for the first time.
I'd let the storm wet my hair,
and pretend that the raindrop
dripping from my cheek was a tear.
I'd pretend I had something to cry about,
just in hopes to feel so deeply again.

It's the cost of being alive,
of living and not just surviving.

If I was sent back to Earth for a day,
I would not visit my own grave.
I'd watch the birds in the trees,
and count every last freckle on me.

I wouldn't want to speak to anyone,
just listen to the way their voice changes when
they start talking about the things they love.
I'd memorize every smile, and sparkle in their
eye.
Only then, in peace could I lie.

Be Patient with Yourself

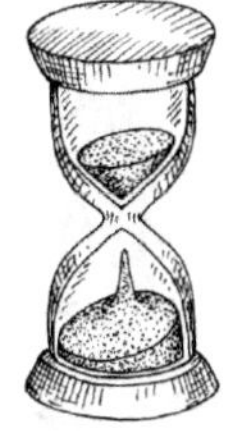

There's only so much tending you can do
to try to heal an open wound.
They say time heals everything,
but never so soon.

My Way

It is cruel how time corrupts us.
Wrinkles on our cheeks,
from the dried-up laughter of our youth.
I just wish I could shake my 10-year-old self,
and tell her that she was right about everything.
She was right that sharing is caring.
She was right that love always wins.
About sleepovers and singing, she was right!

That childlike spark of excitement,
the blissful ignorance,
there's a reason people so desperately
try to cling onto their youth.
But the beauty in getting older,
is getting to fully live out your truth.

Still I hold my younger self dear,
I think of her often and hold her memory near.
There's something to be proud of in that you
have survived every struggle,
to live as long as you have today.
22 years, and I wouldn't have done it any other
way than my way.

Moving on.

And I just hope you know,
this was never the way I wanted things to go.
If you left it to me,
I'd sail across all 7 seas,
and climb to every mountain peak,
if that would get you to believe.

But you told me what's better off dead,
is better off buried,
and handed me the shovel.
Then all it took was the look on your face,
that was my fall from grace.
Never saw this one coming.

Useless.

I'll let you play the victim since you do it so
well.
Faking smiles, pleasantries pretended,
choking on the watered down truth you tell.
Normally I'd be more offended,
but we both have met the real you.

So I wanted to know,
when you hear my name,
is there any pinch of shame?

And when you called me useless,
who am I to you to be used?

To the Other Woman.

Congratulations, you won him,
only at the cost of a sister.

Congratulations, you won him,
only at the price of your pride.

Congratulations, what a prize,
someone who'd throw away unconditional love
for a good night.

Ten years older but not wiser, so let me remind
you.
Sometimes life isn't about winning,
it's about knowing when to admit:
That you've sacrificed far too much already,
That you've compromised every last one
of your morals.
And that a man who doesn't even respect
his own mother, or lover,
will never, ever,
respect
you.

Abundance

I wish I had known back then,
that there really is enough love to go around.
You were not the last person to wish me sweet
dreams,
and my cold hand has been held again,
all the heartbreak is not so lonely as it seems.

And the friends you lose weren't meant to stay,
like the sun, you will meet again another day.
But for now there are new people to meet,
and foreign lands to see.

Love is actually in everything we do,
if you look hard enough.
And if you believe,
it will never stop coming back to you.

Leave the Side Door Cracked.

For love.
It does come again.
Humans are meant to be deeply touched
by many people in our lives.

But you must leave the side door cracked open,
with the porch light left on.

Living Dead.

You must appreciate then, at least,
how much it took to feel anything at all.
There are many zombies walking among us.
Too scared to feel any emotion they'd rather feel
none.

Don't let them turn you, don't believe them
when they say the world has gotten cold,
or that there's no beauty in getting old.
Or that you must show no face,
love at the slowest pace,
deny yourself the right
to live fully.

In a world that wants you to be hard,
stay soft but strong,
and if you follow your heart,
you'll never go wrong.

Phantom Connections.

Best regards to any man who dare comes in
with pure intentions and love to give,
I know right now that in my heart
there's no room for another to live.
Because we aged less like wine, more like
winter,
and the girl you met in November
still wonders if you've missed her.

So every time my vision gets blurry
and the room starts to spin,
I look for the nearest man with your same baggy
eyes, cheek creases when you smile,
and I'll consider that a win.

I'll even let him into my home,
my bed and sheets,
but then when he gets too close,
I'll say it's time to leave.
Because I'm a terrible host.
And a hopeless lover,
tethered to another.

And it does me no good,
comparing every first date's flowers to the taste
of our last kiss.

Both sweet but only one do I miss.
Since it's every candle light dinner that makes
me more of a sinner.

So when someone asks why I think I'm better
off alone, it's because I know,
They deserve someone who isn't destined to
break their hearts,
trying to heal her own.

Narcissus.

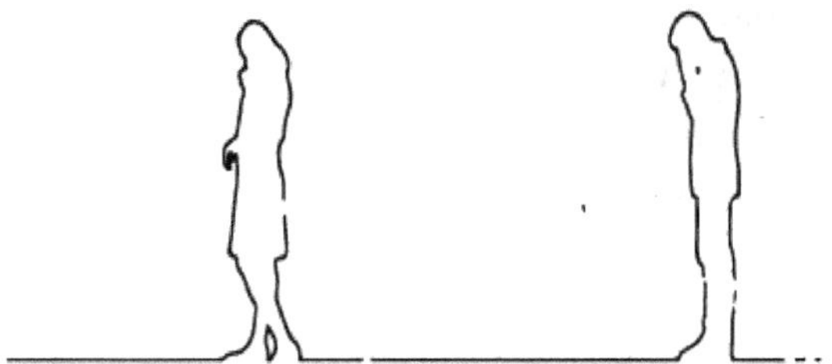

It took me months to realize
that there's nothing beautiful or poetic about
getting the guy who doesn't care about anything
to care about me.

There's nothing romantic about apology flowers,
nothing self righteous having to explain
every little detail of how he hurt me,
just so he'd believe that he did.

I always adored the girls who sang at the top of
their lungs in the middle of the bar,
or the boys who go on for a little too long
talking about their favorite hobbies.
Who wants to love in secret anyways?

So as hard as it is,
you need to believe him when he shows you
who he is.
And when he says "I don't deserve you."
Listen.
Leave.

People don't change overnight, or in two weeks.
Please know that anything worthwhile will be
purposeful, intentional, and done
wholeheartedly.

Isn't it Shameful?

52

How you'll dive head first into
every curve and crevice of her body,
but won't even dip a toe
into the depths of her soul?

Defenses.

And everyone can see my broken heart
because it's falling off my sleeve.

Memory.

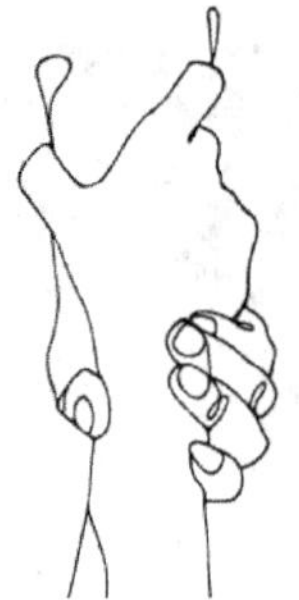

Your name will always mean something
when I hear it in random conversation.
And seeing the sandwich I'd buy for you on my
walk home,
flashback to the way you'd hold me
when we were alone.

You seem to be at the heart of my every
memory.
But it's more of a lingering sort of haunting,
like you with all your taunting.
I deserved a better memory
than what you left me with.

And I will always have love for you,
even if I no longer feel it rushing in my blood.
So can you just let me rest,
knowing that you were loved?

Sad Song Writers Club.

I think maybe I'm just not the type of person
that others fall in love with.
And maybe that's why I'm a poet.

Not to be misleading,
I've made blissful connections,
real fairytale stories,
ones I'll cherish forever.
But love?
That dire thirst?
I don't think I know that.

The ink drips from my pen,
and all that's left is a blubbering mess.

Tried and True.

56

But at the end of the day,
the tried and true from history remains,
love always survives,
and heartbreak hurts the same.
Through everything, this bond persists.
It's the most sour and bittersweet tradeoff,
that no man can resist.

Do Not Disturb.

So if one night in ten months,
four hours you lie there awake,
and you realize that you might actually miss me.

Just know I've been there,
It's a pain that we share.
You will get through it,
but don't reach out to me.

In Another Universe.

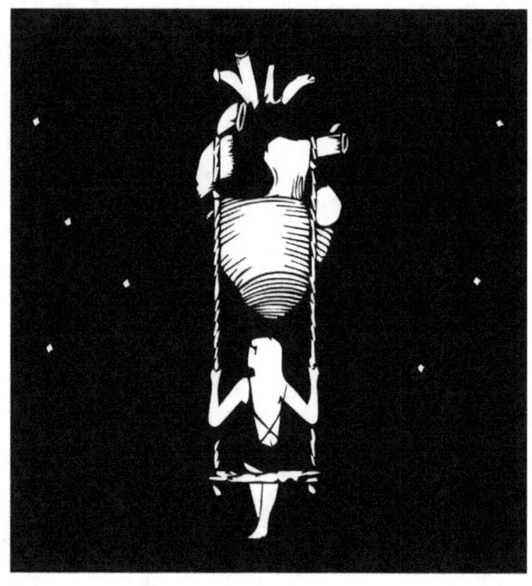

There is no noise,
wrapped arm in arm, chest to chest,
you once told me that you've never known
a quiet, quite like this one.
I always thought I knew you best.

In another universe,
there is no sight
that could ever take your eyes off of me.
There is no touch
that could ever make you feel as free.

There is somewhere far out there,
deep in the cosmos,
where I'm sure that you're perfect for me.
So I take comfort only in knowing,
this will not be the last time that
our souls will meet.
In another universe.

Benefit of Doubt.

I believe people are inherently good,
like without the strain of society,
people would be kind and easy to each other.
Or without the weight of our past,
and carrying the ache of something that should
have last.

And it might be the very thing that gets me
killed.
But I can't help this little lingering feeling deep
inside, that tells me we're all not that different.

I expected more
because it's what I would do, fitted in their
shoes.
It's a reflection of me, not just you.
I must believe people are inherently good.
Because I am people,
and I am good.

Homeland.

What makes a homeland?
Who makes a homeland?
Is it the baker on the corner of Main Street,
that feeds the stray dogs everyday after work,
even when he's feeling defeat?
Or the birds who dance and sing,
gathering together to soar the sky,
in their very own community?
What about the children that put on their holiday
recital every year?
Oblivious, with their tiny shoes and big smiles,
ready to entertain their families for a while.

Who makes a homeland?
Is it the town's single mothers?
Your best friend's big brother?
A distant memory?
A destroyed sanctuary?

Who makes a homeland?
And more importantly,
who decides that it gets taken away
or when it's their last day?

Neighborhood, A Tribute to Bisan

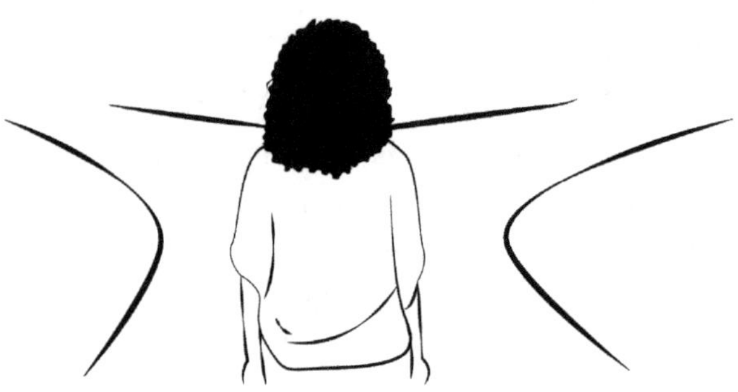

There's a new family in the neighborhood,
with beautiful brown skin, curly hair.
Around the mom's neck a keffiyeh,
neat and clean and tucked with care.

You ask about their home.
They say you wouldn't recognize it.
It's filled with olive trees, and a big blue sea,
but one that is not free.

You ask about their childhood.
They say "short lived,"
a fight for survival,
full of songs of resistance.

How do you welcome that to your
neighborhood?
It's love thy neighbor, no?
Even if thy neighbor is from across the sea?
What about with compassion, sympathy?
With patience, because time is a gift few receive.

What about with nothing less,
than sheer, unabashed, humanity?

Bystander.

When your grandkids ask you what it was like,
the struggle, the fight.
Will you tell them you remained silent?
That it was deafening?
Will you tell them all about it?
The letters you never sent?
The protests you never attend?
The words you never spoke,
or the ones you never meant?

History will always remember complicity.
Your silence will echo in many memories.
It's not your fault you were made a bystander,
but it's up to us now to hold each other
to a higher standard.

Revolution.

People naturally want to resist change.
It is never easy, in anything.
Change, it deconstructs you.
But please know, anything that you once were,
you can build again.
The same with society,
too scared to rewrite history
that we stopped writing.
Is it dangerous to strive for utopia?
Or is it worse to stop striving for anything at all?

My Best Friend

There is something so cherishable
about such a pure friendship,
one you can feel in your bones.

As if it dates back centuries,
a bond so strong.
She'd stand by you in arms
if you were wronged.

Throughout your life you will always expect to
find more of these people,
but when you look back,
it's really only a few,
that you happened to meet at just the perfect
time,
but still so long overdue.

Not Just a Cliché.

I think perhaps the greatest tragedy of
the entire universe,
is that nobody will ever truly know
just how much they are loved.

Like the cashier who complimented my shirt,
how I thought well of him the rest of the day.
Or all my old friends from my childhood,
how I wish we had five more minutes to play.

The old school teacher who let me sleep,
my ex's mother who poured us tea,
all the younger versions of me,

I think we are always far more loved
than we are led to believe.

Compassion, Inspired by Miller Williams.

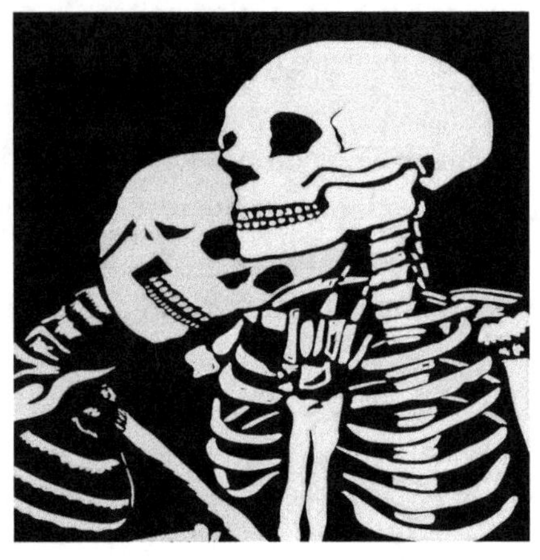

You can still have a profoundly deep love for
this Earth,
while also realizing how harsh it can be.
It is the ultimate price of life.
We just want to live for what we love,
and to live well.

Everyone knows this world is unjust, corrupt.
What it's like to lie awake, contemplating fate.
Understand, this world leaves no soul
untouched.
There is no heart that does not break.

So have compassion,
for every person you meet.
You might not be able to change the world
whole,
but you can for just one night,
for at least one soul.

Spoiler.

I hate endings.
There could never be so many answers,
to even begin asking all the questions I have.
There is never so much closure
that I wouldn't beg for another second.

Everything just feels so final, so complete.

I've always hated endings,
sometimes when I was younger,
I would look up the spoiler to a movie while
watching it.
I didn't want to get too attached to anybody
knowing that they would die.
And I didn't want to be tricked
into rooting for the bad guy.

Spoiler.
What I didn't see coming is that
I was erasing half the story that way.
You cannot simply live your life trying to only
experience the good parts on any given day.

The heartbreak is as deserving as the love,
simply an emotion begging to be heard.
And this is one of the hardest things to learn,

to let it burn, let it burn.

Then at my end,
I can rest peacefully knowing I experienced it
all.
The highs and lows, the climb *and* the fall.
I've lived fully and ran when my passions
called.

And that, fall and all, is a life well lived.

You and Me and Mother Earth.

I do not know which sacred text I believe but the
soil,
and the holy land between you and me.
It is to the Earth that I am loyal,
it is to her I wish to please.

Is it not her trees that give me
the oxygen that I breathe?
Is it not her plentiful fruit,
that we pick and pluck, prying from their root,
that she keeps on giving?

Do the stars not map out the entire galaxy?
Does the sun not shine every day,
for both you and me?
For if there is a God, she is here on Earth.
Marveling at her creations,
and learning her worth.